Praying with the Saints

Saints' lives and prayers

Praying with the Saints

Saints' lives and prayers

VERITAS

First published 1987 by
William Lane SJ
Lusaka

This edition published 1989 by
Veritas Publications
7/8 Lower Abbey Street
Dublin 1

Copyright © William Lane SJ

ISBN 1 85390 034 6

Cover design by Jim Kilgarriff
Typesetting by Printset & Design Ltd, Dublin
Printed in the Republic of Ireland by
The Leinster Leader

Contents

What is a saint?	5
Aelred	7
Ambrose	9
Anselm	10
Augustine	14
Basil	22
Bede	24
Benedict	25
Bernard	26
Bernardine	28
Bonaventure	29
Catherine of Siena	30
Clement	32
Columbanus	34
Cyril	35
Dionysius	36
Francis de Sales	38
Francis of Assisi	40
Gregory	42
Hilary	44
Ignatius	45
Jerome	48
John Chrysostom	49
John Fisher	50
John Vianney	52
Patrick	53
Peter Canisius	55
Polycarp	58
Richard	58
Teresa	59
Thomas Aquinas	63
Thomas More	65

What is a saint?

Saints are not angels. Nor are they plaster statues with smooth, unlined faces. They are human beings, flesh and blood creatures who entered the world with particular characters and temperaments. They were in a way larger than life but they also lost their tempers, got angry, scolded God or were irritable and difficult to live with.

The art of writing the lives of saints is too often pious rather than stirring and inspiring. Very often these fine people, often born with the same obstacles to virtue as ourselves, are held up for display as something more than human as if they were creatures from another planet. They seem never to have sinned, stumbled or faltered. As children they seem to have been good, never to have had any trouble in adolescence and to have been saints by the time they were middle-aged. To paint the saints this way is to tell the story of a life without struggle and without any inspiration or help for ordinary people.

Yet more than 300 years ago St Francis de Sales warned that we should not read sanctity into every act of a canonised saint. 'There is', he wrote 'no harm to the saints if their faults are shown as well as their virtues, but great harm is done to everybody by those historians who gloss over the faults, whether for the purpose of honouring the saints or through fear of lessening our reverence for their holiness.' It is much more profitable to honour a person grown good by his efforts than one who had no struggle.

So what is a saint? A human being certainly, but with some kind of added dimension, rather like an artist or a poet or a musician. There is in them all a kind of obsession, preoccupation, genius that makes them totally absorbed by something. With the artist it is a vision of colour, form, line; with the poet it is language, atmosphere; with the musician it is sound, harmony. With the saint it is God and goodness, and the fact that to do what God wants is the supreme thing in life. Like the artist, the poet, the musician, the saints used ordinary means to complete their masterpieces.

For the saint, therefore, life is being caught up in doing what God wants. We try to do this also but the monotony and routine of ordinary living erode our efforts so that we seek God in bits and not constantly. The saint constantly uses every opportunity, often the same as ours, to do the best thing. He or she turns every impulse towards God and is constantly drawn by him and longs for him with no let-up in a selfless search that is led by the Spirit.

One of the most noticeable things about the saints is that they channelled their thirst for God into caring for the necessities close to hand — healing the sick and the lepers; feeding the poor and the needy; preaching the word of God to as many people as possible; providing education for the unlettered. Because they were totally absorbed with God, they were also totally absorbed with his creatures.

The saints were joyous realists. Much is written today about self-acceptance and feeling good about oneself. The saints, as seen in their prayers, accepted themselves as sinners and knew that they were accepted by God for what they were. They stood in complete sincerity before God and believed deeply that growth and success were from him who was behind and beneath all their strivings. Their lives were thus filled with great joy. St Teresa wrote that she believed joy to be as essential to holiness as good works.

The prayers in this little book have been gathered together to give some idea of how the saints prayed and what they prayed for — they praised God, thanked him, longed for him, complained to him, apologised to him, talked to him as a friend and they prayed to him for themselves, for other people whether sinners or close friends, for a knowledge and acceptance of themselves, for protection, strength, courage, faith, perseverance. In short they prayed as loved creatures standing before God, constantly aware of their position as his children and the great permanent needs of people of all times and cultures.

The saints are very much alive today. They are a part of the Church that has reached full perfection in heaven. There they see us as they once were, pilgrims on the way. We rely for help on their prayers to God, the prayers of a huge army of martyrs, doctors of the Church, hermits, founders of orders, married men and women, virgins, witnesses to the faith. They pray that we may persevere in faith, hope and love so that where they are we may one day be.

Aelred

Aelred was born in Hexham in England in 1109. At an early age he was taken into the service of King David of Scotland. When he was twenty-four, after an inner struggle, he entered the Cistercian monastery of Rievlaux in Yorkshire, England. In 1147 he became abbot of this monastery which prospered under his guidance, with the numbers increasing to 650, which made Rievlaux the largest monastery of that time in England.

Aelred, although delicate, was an energetic and compassionate man. His name is particularly associated with friendship, both human and divine. His position as abbot involved travelling on visitation to Cistercian monasteries throughout England and in Europe. He died in Rievlaux in 1167.

The value Aelred placed on friendship appears in his writings which are characterised by a constant appeal to Christ as a friend and saviour. The best known of his works are *A Mirror of Charity* and *On Spiritual Friendship — Sermons on Isaiah*.

Acceptance, Forgiveness, Strength

Please look at me, dear Lord.
In your merciful and loving kindness
is my hope, for you see me
just as a good doctor,
anxious only to heal and correct.
This I ask you, kind Lord,
trusting in your powerful mercy
and your merciful power.
Forgive my sins;
rouse me from my half-heartedness;
forget my ingratitude.
I acknowledge in myself
those voices and evil passions
which still fight within me,
whether due to long-standing evil habits
or carelessness repeated every day
or deep-seated flaws of my weak nature
or hardly recognised temptings
of evil spirits.

Against all these enemies
may your gentle grace
give me strength and courage.

Ambrose

The son of a French army officer, Ambrose was born in Trier about 334. While practising law in the Roman courts, he was appointed about 370 as governor of the province whose capital was Milan in Italy. In 374, even though only a catechumen, he was by popular request chosen as bishop of Milan. This city had its problems, for it was the administrative centre of the western part of the Roman Empire which meant that its bishop had no choice but to be involved in politics. Ambrose influenced the Roman Emperor not to allow the restoration of pagan statues and to do public penance for murdering Christians. In 386 he baptised St Augustine. He died in Milan in 397.

Ambrose valued highly the instruction of people, mostly through sermons and doctrinal writings that were aimed at applying scripture to life. He was the first to use hymns in church as a means of praising God and instructing people.

For a loving heart

Lord, you are merciful;
take away my sins from me
and give me the graces
of your Holy Spirit.
Take away from me
this heart of stone

and give me a heart
of flesh and blood
to love and adore you,
to delight in you,
to please you,
for the sake of Christ.

To Christ our strength

Lord Jesus Christ, you are
medicine when I am sick,
strength when I need help,
life when I fear death,
the way when I long for heaven,
the light when all is dark,
my food when I need nourishment.

For protection

Be gracious to our prayers, O God,
and guard your people
with loving protection;
that they who confess
your Son as God,
born a human being like us,
may never be corrupted
by the deceits of the devil
through Jesus Christ, our Lord.

Anselm

Anselm was born in Aosta in Italy in 1033. After a restless youth he entered a monastery in 1059. For thirty years he wrote philosophical and theological works that had great influence on the teaching of the Church. He became abbot of his monastery in 1078. In 1093 King William II of England nominated him Archbishop of Canterbury. From this on, much of his time was taken up with the disagreements between William II and Henry I over relations between Church and State, centred mainly on the election of bishops without interference from the king. Anselm spent the years 1097–1100 in Rome and returned to England when Henry I became king. But disputes arose again and Anselm found himself in exile once more from 1103–1107. He died in Canterbury in 1109.

A value which stands out in Anselm's writings is the clear understanding and elaboration of the truth which his heart believed and loved. He valued the individual and his freedom as may be seen from his opposition to slavery. A man of charming personality, he was more at home as a monk in the monastery than as a statesman at the court of the king.

For friends

O Blessed Lord,
you have commanded us
to love one another.
You have freely given us
many gifts of body and soul.
Give us the grace
that in loving you
and for your sake,
we may love everyone else
in the whole world.
We ask your mercy for all,
but especially for our friends

that your love has given us.
Love them, O Fountain of love,
and make them love you with all their hearts
so that they may will,
speak and do
only those things
that are pleasing to you.

Seeking God

O Lord, our God,
grant us the grace to long for you
with our whole heart,
and that so longing
we may seek and find you;
and that so finding you
we may love you;
and that so loving you
we may hate those sins
from which you redeemed us
for the sake of Jesus Christ.

For the suffering

We bring before you, Lord,
the troubles and dangers
of people and nations;
the sighing of prisoners,
the sorrows of the bereaved,
the necessities of strangers,
the dependency of the weary,
the failing powers of the aged,
Lord, draw near to each
for the sake of Jesus Christ.

To the Holy Spirit

O Holy Spirit,
consolation of the sorrowful,
come down to us at this time
with your mighty power
into the depths of our hearts.
Gladden there with your brightness
every dark corner
and make all rich with your comfort.
Give us inner warmth
that our prayers and praises
may always go up to you, our God,
through Jesus Christ,
your Son our Lord.

For help to live well

Merciful Father,
in the beginning you created us
and by the Passion of your only Son
you created us anew.
Work in us now, we ask you,
both to will and do what pleases you.
Since we are weak and of ourselves
can do no good,
grant us your grace and heavenly blessing
that in whatever work we are engaged
we may do all for your honour and glory;
that being kept from sin
and growing in doing good
so long as we live on this earth
we may serve you;

and after our death
we may be forgiven all our sins
and attain eternal life.

Desire for God

I ask you, O kind God,
never desert me as I call on you,
for before I searched for you,
you were already searching for me.
You wanted me to search for you,
to find you and to love you,
I looked for you and found you, Lord,
and now I want to love you.
Increase that desire in me
and grant what I ask,
for if all that I ask were given
it would not be enough without you.
Give me then yourself, Lord,
for I love you and my love is strong,
even though it is very little.

Augustine

Augustine was born in Numidia in 354 and lived for some time in Algeria in North Africa. His father was a pagan and his mother, Monica, a Christian. At sixteen he went to Carthage to finish his education and lived there with a woman for fourteen years. He had a son called Adeodatus. After his studies, he found it hard to settle down to teaching, searching as he was for a philosophy of life. By 383 he was lecturing in Rome after which he went to Milan, where he was influenced by the preaching and friendship of St Ambrose, who was bishop of Milan. He struggled within himself. On the one side he was pulled by a life of honour, wealth and marriage and on the other by a life given totally and directly to God. He had tried vice and it offered no peace. He longed to be delivered from his degenerate way of life, worldliness, laziness, softness, irregular sexual behaviour and all those perennial sins that split and scatter the efforts of people aspiring to be good. He kept putting off the decision with words, as he writes in his *Confessions,* 'By and by, let me alone a little longer, chastity but not yet'. But God kept after him and he made his decision one day in a garden when he read Romans 13: 12-14. 'The night is nearly over, day is almost here. Let us stop doing the things that belong to the dark, and let us take up weapons for fighting in the light. Let us conduct ourselves properly, as people who live in the light of day — no orgies or drunkenness, no immorality or indecency, no fighting or jealousy. But take up the weapons of the Lord Jesus Christ, and stop paying attention to your sinful nature and satisfying its desire'. In 391 he was ordained priest and in 396 became Bishop of Hippo. He was bishop for thirty-four years until his death in 410.

Augustine's chief values were the good administration of his diocese, and writing to correct the errors of his time and explain the great doctrines of Christianity — the Trinity and grace. He wrote commentaries on the Psalms and the Gospels but is perhaps best known for the story of his spiritual voyage of discovering God — the *Confessions,* in which with perfect honesty he tries to set down his total journey to God.

Trust

All-powerful God,
you care for each one of us
as if you loved him alone
and you care for all
as if all were only one.
Things of this world pass away
that others may replace them;
But you never pass away or depart.
O God our Father, supremely good,
beauty of all things beautiful,
to you we entrust
whatever we have received from you,
through Jesus Christ our Lord.

Night prayer

Watch, Lord, with those who wake
or watch or weep tonight,
and give your angels charge
over those who sleep.
Tend your sick ones, O Lord Christ;
rest your weary ones;
bless your dying ones;
soothe your suffering ones;
pity your afflicted ones;
shield your joyous ones;
and all for your love's sake.

For forgiveness

Lord Jesus Christ,
for the sake of your holy name,
for the sake of your bitter passion,

for the sake of your great mercy,
forgive and forget what I have been;
pity what I am;
satisfy for what I deserve;
grant what I ask.
You looked for me, O Lord,
when I fled from you.
Will you reject me now
that I look for you?

Protection in life's journey

Blessed are all your saints, O God and King,
who have travelled the stormy sea of this life
and have made the harbour of peace and
happiness.
Watch over us who are still on our dangerous voyage,
and remember those exposed to the rough
storms of trouble and temptations.
Our ship is frail and the ocean is wide;
but in your mercy you have set our course
to steer our ship of life
towards the everlasting shore of peace
and bring us at last to the quiet haven
of our heart's desire
where you, O God, are blessed
and live and reign for ever and ever.

Seeking God

Look on us, O Lord,
and let the darkness of our souls vanish
before the rays of your brightness.

Fill us with love and open to us
the treasures of your wisdom.
All our wishes are known to you;
make perfect, therefore,
what you have already begun
and what your Holy Spirit
has moved us to ask in prayer.
We seek your face;
turn to us and show us your glory,
then all our longing will be satisfied
and our peace will be perfect
through Jesus Christ our Lord.

For a friend

Lord Jesus Christ,
give to my friend
a heart to love you;
a will to choose you;
a memory to remember you;
a mind to think of you;
a soul united to you.
And may you,
God of love and mercy,
love him for ever and ever.

Praise

You are great, O Lord,
and greatly to be praised.
Your power is great.
Your wisdom is limitless.

Help us to praise you without end.
You call on us to delight in your praise
for you have made us for yourself
and our hearts are restless
until they rest in you,
who with the Father and the Holy Spirit,
all honour and glory are due,
now and forever.

To Mary, mother of the Church

Mary, gracious Lady,
you are mother and virgin.
You are mother of the body and soul
of our Head and Redeemer.
You are also truly our mother,
of all the members of Christ's Body.
For through your love
you have helped to bring to birth
the faithful in the Church.
Unique among women,
you are mother and virgin,
mother of Christ and virgin of Christ.
You are the beauty and charm of earth;
you are forever the image of the Church.
Through a woman came death;
through a woman came life.
Yes, through you, O mother of God.

Searching for God

Too late have I loved you,
O beauty always old and ever new.
Behold you were within

and I looked for you elsewhere
and in my weakness
I ran after the beauty
in the things you had made.
You were with me
and I was not with you.
The things you created kept me from you.
You have called
and have pierced my deafness.
You have shone out
and have lifted my blindness.
You have sent out your sweetness
and I have longed after you
and looked for you,
I have tasted you
and hungered after you.
And now my whole hope
is in nothing else
but in your great mercy
O Lord, my God.

The Holy Spirit

Breathe into me, Holy Spirit,
that my mind may turn to what is holy.
Move me, Holy Spirit,
that I may do what is holy.
Strengthen me, Holy Spirit,
that I may preserve what is holy.
Protect me, Holy Spirit,
that I may never lose what is holy.

That we may share with others

O Lord and Saviour, you have told us
that you will ask much of those
to whom much has been given.
Grant that we, who have received much,
may work together all the harder,
by prayer, almsgiving, fasting
and every other way given to us
to share with others what we enjoy.
And as we have enjoyed the fruits
of the labours of other people
may we so work that they may enjoy
the fruits of our labours,
so as to please you
and help towards our own salvation
through Jesus Christ our Lord.

To serve the needs of others

Lord, although rich,
for our sakes you became poor
and promised in your gospel
that whatever is done
to the least of your brothers
is done to you.
Give us the grace, we humbly ask,
to be always willing and ready
to serve the needs of other people
and to spread the blessings
of your Kingdom
all over the world
to your praise and glory.

For God's help in everything

God, from whom to be turned is to fall;
to whom to be turned is to rise;
and in whom to stand is to live forever:
grant us
in all our duties your help,
in all our problems your guidance,
in all our dangers your protection,
in all our sorrows your peace,
through Jesus Christ our Lord.

Basil

Basil, known as the Great, was born in Caesarea in Cappadocia about 330. He came from an old, well-known Christian family.

He was educated in Caesarea, Constantinople and Athens. About 357 he visited the chief monasteries of the east and settled as a monk in Pontus, where he remained for five years. From 365, having been ordained priest, he was responsible for the diocese of Caesarea and was made bishop there. As bishop he had to stand up against the persecution of eastern Christians by the Emperor Valens. His headstrong approach to these controversies led him into many difficulties. St Basil died in Caesarea in 379.

Basil valued highly eastern monasticism which is still influenced by the principles he laid down. Most of his time and energy was spent in successfully fighting the heresy of Arianism. A work he valued highly was the provision of a church, a hospital and dwelling houses for the sick and the poor. He spoke out boldly against the vices of the rich. He wrote many letters and sermons and it is from these that most of the information about his life comes.

For others
Remember, Lord, all those
who call on your loving kindness,
our friends and our enemies
and all those who have asked us
to pray for them.
Remember, O Lord our God,
all our children.
Let them know
how great is your mercy
and give them
all that is for their good.
Remember, Lord, all
who are unknown to us
or are forgotten by us,
for you know each one by name
and all the years of their lives
even from their mother's womb.

That we may live well
Teach us, O Lord,
to pray for the right blessings.
Guide our ship of life towards yourself,
you calm port of storm-tossed souls.
Show us the course we should follow
and renew a willing spirit within us.

Let your Spirit curb our wandering senses
and guide us to that which is our true good,
to keep your laws and in all our deeds
to rejoice always in your glorious presence.
For yours is the glory and the praise
from all your saints forever and ever.

Hope

O God, you are
the hope of the hopeless,
the saviour of the troubled,
the healer of the sick.
Be to us all things for all
for you know each one singly,
the prayer and need of each,
the home of each.

Bede

Bede was born in Northumbria in England in 673. He became a monk and a priest in the school where he received his early education. During his whole life he never moved very far from his monastery, where most of his time was spent writing about the Scriptures. But he is best remembered for his history of the English Church and people. He also wrote grammars and hymns. Bede died in 735.

In his own words his values were 'the study of the Scriptures, observing monastic discipline, and singing the daily services in church; study and teaching have always been my delight'.

God's will – our life

Open our hearts, O Lord,
and enlighten us
by the grace of the Holy Spirit
that we may seek
what is pleasing to your will
and so order our lives
according to your commandments
that we may be found worthy
to enter your unending joys
through Jesus Christ our Lord.

Benedict

Benedict was born in Umbria in Italy about 480. Little is known of his life. He went to Rome for liberal studies, but life there was so bad that, when he was about twenty, he fled to the mountains and became a hermit at Subiaco about fifty kilometres from Rome. He spent three years contemplating in solitude and then organised others who wished to join him into twelve small communities. In 529 he set up the famous monastery of Monte Cassino. Here he lived a life of prayer and solitude. Many came to him for spiritual direction. While at Monte Cassino he drew up a set of rules for those who were living in the community with him. He died at Monte Cassino about 547.

'The Holy Rule' which Benedict wrote shows how much he valued peace, reflection on life and moderation. He combined a love of discipline with respect for people's personalities and talents.

A life turned towards God

O gracious and holy Father, give us
wisdom to perceive you,
intelligence to understand you,
diligence to seek you,
patience to wait for you,
eyes to behold you,
a heart to meditate on you,
and a life to proclaim you
through the power of the spirit
of Jesus Christ our Lord.

Bernard

Bernard was born in Dijon in France in 1090 and was one of six sons of a Burgundian nobleman. In 1113 he joined a monastery at Citeaux and persuaded four of his brothers and twenty-seven friends to join him. In 1115 he was sent to set up a new monastery at Clairvaux. He played a large part in the foundation of the Cistercian Order. Clairvaux grew and was the origin of sixty-eight other houses. Bernard took part in controversies and reforms — the disputed papal election of 1130, the contest with Peter Abelard, luxury among the clergy and the Roman curia, persecution of the Jews. He was commissioned to stir up enthusiasm for the second crusade in France and Germany. This crusade was not a success and Bernard received much abuse for having recommending it. He died at Clairvaux in 1153.

One of Bernard's prime values was extensive use of scripture in writings and preaching, 'not so much in order to expound the words as to reach people's hearts'. This affective use of scripture in preaching and writing is something that is very contemporary and makes Bernard a man for our times.

Bernard also valued involvement in the application of spiritual principles to public office, dealing with corruption, nepotism and other abuses of position.

Bernard's main writings were *A Life of St Malachy of Armagh* and *On the Love of God*.

A prayer of confidence to Our Lady

Remember, O most gracious Virgin Mary,
that never was it known
that anyone who fled to your protection,
implored your help,
or sought your intercession
was left unaided.
Filled with this confidence
we fly to your help
O virgin of virgins our mother.
To you we come,
before you we stand
sinful and sorrowful.
Mary, mother of the Word made man,
do not despise our request
but in your mercy
hear and answer us.

Asking Jesus Christ for mercy

We look for you, O Lord,
for the goodness and kindness

we are sure to find in you,
because we know
you did not despise the poor
nor reject the sinner.
You did not reject the good thief
nor the sinful woman who repented,
nor the Canaan mother who prayed to you,
nor the woman taken in adultery,
nor the man who was a tax collector,
nor the publican who asked forgiveness,
nor the disciple who denied you,
nor even those who killed you.
It is such forgiveness
that draws us back to you.

Bernardine

Bernardine was born in Italy in 1380. As a young man he took charge of the hospital in Siena when most of the staff had been killed by the plague. In 1402 he joined the Franciscans and was ordained in the following year. He soon became famous as a preacher and spent most of his time travelling up and down Italy preaching in churches and in the open. He always travelled on foot and sometimes preached for three or four hours at a time. In 1430 he was obliged to give up his missionary work to become the vicar general of the Friars of the Strict Observance. He was from this time active in the order to restore it to a stricter observance of the rule. In 1442 he received permission from the Pope to resign from the post of vicar general and take up again his missionary journeys, which he loved so well. He took part in the Council of Florence and in 1444 set out on a preaching journey to Naples, but his strength failed and he died on the way.

The prime value in Bernardine's life was the communication of the gospel message through popular preaching. He was known as 'the people's preacher'. While vicar general he constantly longed to be giving his popular missions.

To remove from us what is not God's

O Lord Jesus Christ,
acknowledge in us what is yours
and take away from us
all that is not yours
for your honour and glory.

Bonaventure

Bonaventure was born in Bagnorea in Italy in 1221. He studied at Paris and then joined the Franciscan Order. He preached and lectured for many years in Paris and defended the Franciscans from their attackers. He became the head of the Franciscan order in 1257. In 1273 he became the Cardinal Archbishop of Albano in Italy and attended the Church Council of Lyons. He died during this council and was buried in Lyons in 1274.

Bonaventure valued, as seen in his works, deep understanding of religion, but he valued even more highly the love and knowledge of God that simple people very often have.

Bonaventure wrote many works of philosophy, theology and higher prayer. He also wrote a life of St Francis of Assisi and the well-known *Journey of the soul to God.*

To be washed from sin

Wash me fully from all my sins,
Lord Jesus Christ,
that I may be worthy
to live in your heart
all the days of my life.

Catherine of Siena

Catherine Benincasa was born in Siena, Italy about 1347 and was the youngest of a very large family. A lively, good-looking girl, she resisted her parents' efforts to get her to marry. She led a life of prayer and penance at her home and became a tertiary sister of the Dominican Order. After some years of solitude, she began to mix with other people, first by nursing the sick in hospital and then by gathering a group of disciples around her. These were to accompany her on her later travels and witness some of her conversions of great evil-doers.

Catherine, although illiterate, lectured popes and almost single-handedly brought some peace during wars in Italy. In the last five years of her life she became involved with the politics of both State and Church, when she tried to mediate in the armed conflict between

Florence and other communities and the papal government. When a rival Pope was set up in Avignon, France, in 1378 Catherine wrote often to the Pope in Rome to be less harsh and to many European rulers to recognise the Pope in Rome as being the true Pope. In these discussions she was very outspoken.

She went to live in Rome, but in 1380 suffered a stroke and died eight days later. Although most of the civilised world was affected by her, Catherine hardly ever left home.

Catherine was a woman of great personal sanctity, had many visions and became a person of international importance. She tried to express her ideals in her letters and her main work, *The Dialogue*.

For sinners

To you, Eternal Father,
all is possible.
Although you have created us
without our help
you will not save us
without our help.
I pray you to turn the will
of these sinners, to dispose them
to will as they ought
and as they do not.
I ask it of your infinite mercy.
From nothing you have created us.
Now that we exist, have mercy on us.
Repair the vessels that you have formed
in your own likeness;

restore them to grace, through mercy
and through the blood
of your Son, Jesus Christ.

Our weakness

You see, O Lord,
the law of our perverse nature
always ready to rebel against your will;
but in all things you provide for us
and you have found a remedy for all.
You give us the rock and fortress
of your will to make us strong,
for you allow us to share the strength
of your will to make us strong.

Clement

Very little is known of Clement I who is generally considered to be the third successor of St Peter. St Irenaeus mentions that Clement had associated with the apostles. He is remembered for the letter he sent from the Church of Rome to the Church at Corinth in Greece, where some Corinthian Christians were revolting against the leaders of their Church.

From the letter sent to Corinth we can see that for Clement, pastoral care was an important value.

For truth

God almighty,
Father of our Lord Jesus Christ,
grant us, we ask you,

to be grounded and settled
in your truth
by the coming of the Holy Spirit
into our hearts.
That which we do not know,
reveal to us.
That which is missing in us,
supply to us.
That which we know,
confirm in us
and keep us blameless
in your service
through the same
Jesus Christ our Lord.

Help for the needy

We ask you, Lord and Master,
to be our help and assistance.
Save those who are in trouble;
have mercy on the lonely;
lift up the fallen;
show yourself to the needy;
heal the ungodly;
convert the wanderers;
feed the hungry;
raise up the weak;
comfort the fainthearted.
Let all peoples know
that you are God alone
and Jesus Christ is your Son
and we are your people,
the sheep of your pasture,
for the sake of Jesus Christ.

Columbanus

Columbanus was born in Leinster, Ireland, about 540 and became a monk at an early age. When he was about forty-five, he went to the continent of Europe where he proved to be one of the most influential monks from Ireland. With twelve companions he founded three monasteries in France and later others throughout Europe. He did not adapt very well the austere Irish penitential customs to the continent of Europe and this aroused criticism. He incurred the enmity of Queen Brunhild by his criticism of the loose lifestyle of her nephew. In 610 Columbanus and his Irish monks were ordered to be deported, but they escaped into northern Italy in 612. He founded the famous monastery at Bobbio in 614, where he died the following year.

Columbanus valued highly the strict monastic life.

For revelation that leads to love

I beg you, most loving Saviour,
to reveal yourself to us who ask you,
so that knowing you we may
love you alone,
contemplate you alone
by day and by night
and ever hold you in our thoughts.
Fill us with your love
as is fitting for you to be loved
and honoured as our God,
so that love may fill
the inner depths of our being
and your love may own us all

and your affection may fill
all our senses
so that we may know no other love
apart from you who lives for ever and ever.

For the water of life

Lord, you are the fountain
always to be desired
and always to be drunk.
Give us always, Lord Christ,
this water that it may be in us
a fountain of water
that lives and springs up
to eternal life.

Cyril

Cyril was born in Alexandria about 380. In 412 he succeeded his uncle as bishop of that city. His rule at the beginning was somewhat harsh. He caused the churches of a sect called the Novations to be closed and drove out the Jews, which angered the governor. In 428 Nestorious became Archbishop of Constantinople and began to teach that in Christ there were two distinct persons. He was an outstanding theologian who rendered a lasting service to Christianity by defending the unity of Christ's person at the Council of Ephesus in 431. In the years after the Council, Cyril was less extreme in his efforts to reconcile those who were in error. He died in Alexandria in 444.

Cyril valued highly orthodox teaching about Christ and spent much of his time and energy in writing about this.

For love of other people

O God of love,
you have given us a new commandment,
through your only begotten Son,
that we should love one another
even as you have loved us,
the unworthy and the wandering,
and gave your Son
for our life and salvation.
We pray you to give us
in all the time of our life here,
a mind forgetful of past ill-will,
a pure conscience,
sincere thoughts,
and a heart to love other people
for the sake of Jesus Christ
your Son, our Lord and Saviour.

Dionysius

Dionysius was the head of a catechetical school for about fourteen years. In 247 he was made Bishop of Alexandria. He was arrested during the persecutions that soon broke out there but he escaped and directed his Church from a hiding place in the Libyan desert until the persecuting emperor died in 251. There was much debate about those who had fallen away during the persecution. Dionysius favoured lenient treatment for them after they had repented. Further persecution broke out in Alexandria and Dionysius was once again arrested. His seventeen years as bishop were disturbed by continual persecution, yet he took a very active part in Church affairs.

Dionysius greatly valued the writing of doctrinal truths, although few of his writings have been preserved.

For unity

O God the Father,
good beyond all that is good,
fair beyond all that is fair,
in whom is calmness,
peace and harmony;
make up the divisions
which keep us apart
and bring us back
into a unity of love
which may bear some likeness
to your divine nature.
And as you are above all things
make us one
by the unity of a good mind,
that through charity and affection
we may be spiritually one
as in each other,
through that peace of yours
which makes all things peaceful,
and through the grace,
mercy and tenderness
of your Son, Jesus Christ.

Francis de Sales

St Francis de Sales was born in Lyons, France in 1567. He studied at Paris and Padua in Italy. He was, despite opposition from his father, ordained a priest in 1593. His first work, lasting four years, was to win back to Catholicism the people of his native Chablais country who had gone over to Calvinism. In 1602 Francis became Bishop of Geneva in Switzerland, where he immediately set himself about reforming his new diocese. In 1614, with St Jane de Chantal, he founded the Order of the Visitation. He died in 1622.

Francis, a psychologist, humanist and a very gentlemanly, urbane saint, had as one of his main values in life the possibilities for holiness in ordinary life, in the shop, the office, the home and the school, and this without any kind of exaggeration. There was once an exercise to discover what a saint was, and the subject taken for examination was Francis de Sales. A hole was drilled in the wall of Francis' bedroom so that an observer could spy on Francis when he thought he was alone. All the observer discovered was that Francis in private was exactly the same as he was in company — that he got up early and quietly so as not to wake the servants; that he prayed, wrote and answered letters, read his office, prayed and slept again. There was no secret Francis. The patron saint of journalists and writers, his two best known works are *Introduction to the Devout Life* and *The Love of God*.

To Mary, mother of God

Most holy Mary, virgin mother of God,
although unworthy to be your servant

yet moved by your motherly care for me
and longing to serve you,
I choose you this day
in the presence of my guardian angel
and all the saints in heaven
to be my queen, my helper and my mother
and I firmly resolve to serve you always
and to do what I can that all may
faithfully serve you.
Therefore, most loving mother,
through the precious blood of your Son
poured out for me,
I beg you to receive me
as your servant forever.
Help me in all that I do
and ask for me the grace
never by word, action or thought
to be displeasing to you or your Son.
Remember me and do not leave me
at the hour of my death.

A night prayer

Far from the busy day, I bring you my heart,
I belong to you, my God and Father.
Thank you for keeping me safe today;
thank you for helping me to do good,
I am sorry for the guilt I have earned
by thought, word, deed and negligence.
Help me to do better.
To your care, Lord,
I commend my body and soul,
my relatives, friends and the entire Church.
I go to sleep with your blessing.

One day my last evening will come
when I will enter eternity.
Let me now so live that all I do in time
may be a preparation for this last blessed peace,
that vision may follow faith,
possession succeed hope,
perfect union replace imperfect love,
for you are my final end and greatest good.

Francis of Assisi

Francis was born in Assisi about 1181. The son of a wealthy cloth merchant, as a youth he led a wild life with his friends. An experience of sickness and war matured him. He sold some of his father's cloth to find money to repair the local church. His father disinherited him and sent him away without anything. In 1210 Pope Innocent III authorised him, with eleven companions, to be wandering preachers of Christ. In this way began the Order of Friars Minor or Lesser Brothers. Throughout Italy these brothers, few of whom were priests, preached faith and penance.

In 1212 Francis founded with St Clare the first community of Poor Clares. In 1219 he went with the crusaders to Egypt. By 1217 the movement was beginning to develop into a religious order with many members, provinces and missionaries to countries outside Italy. In 1221 Francis produced a revised version of the rule. Three years later there appeared on his body scars corresponding to the five wounds of Christ. These were a source of constant pain until his death in 1226.

Francis is perhaps one of the best known saints among

Christians of all communions. He valued most highly the single-minded following of Christ in the poverty of the gospel.

His writings include *The Canticle of the Sun, The Little Flowers of St Francis* and *The Mirror of Perfection.*

Praise

Most high, Almighty, Good Lord,
to you be praise, glory, honour
and all blessing.
To you alone, Most High,
they are due
and no one is worthy
to speak your name.

To spread goodness

Lord, make us instruments of your peace,
where there is hatred let us sow love,
where there is injury, pardon,
where there is discord, union,
where there is doubt, faith,
where there is despair, hope,
where there is darkness, light,
where there is sadness, joy,
for your mercy and your truth's sake.

To follow Christ

God Almighty, Eternal,
Righteous and Merciful,

give us poor sinners
to do for your sake
all that we know of your will
and to will always what pleases you
so that inwardly purified,
enlightened and kindled
by the fire of the Holy Spirit,
we may follow in the footsteps
of your Son our Lord Jesus Christ.

Gregory

Gregory, called the Great, was born in Rome about 540 and came from a noble family. For some years he was the chief civil magistrate in the city of Rome. He became a monk when he was about thirty-five. From 579 to 585 he was the Pope's representative in Constantinople and in 590 was himself elected Pope. His fourteen years as Pope were filled with difficulties and disorder. He promoted good relations with the various tribes that were invading Italy and thus strengthened the Church's position. He spent much of the Church's income on the relief of refugees. By his diplomacy, he managed to keep the Church free from civil interference. He also sent missionaries to England. Pope Gregory died in 604.

Gregory wrote much and one of the values appearing in his writings is the formation and education of priests. One of his best known works is *The Dialogues,* an account of the miraculous deeds of holy people in Italy.

Dying to sin, rising to life

O God, to save us you gave your Son
to a painful death on the cross
and by his glorious resurrection
delivered us from the power of the enemy.
Grant us to die daily to sin
that we may live closer to him,
in the joy of the resurrection,
through Christ our Lord.

For the dying

O God, Lord and Creator of all
and especially of mankind;
God, Father and ruler of your children;
judge over life and death;
guardian and helper of our souls;
all things are made by you
and all things are changed by your word,
when the time comes,
according to your wisdom and providence.
Take to yourself now I pray you,
our brother/sister
who goes ahead of us who remain.
Take us also to yourself
in your own good time,
when our given span of life
has been completed.
May the fear of you, O Lord,
make us prepared and yet untroubled,
so that at the time of our death
we shall not hold back and,

unwilling to depart, have to be dragged
and torn from this life,
as people fascinated by this world;
but rather going willingly and readily
to the life of eternal happiness
in Christ Jesus our Lord
to whom be glory forever and ever.

Hilary

Hilary was born about 315 in Poitiers in France and belonged to a well-off pagan family. He was a very cultured man and in time became a Christian. At the age of thirty-five he was elected bishop of Poitiers. He was outstanding for his opposition to the heresy of Arianism. In 356 he was banished by the Arian emperor, but he continued his campaign against the heresy. His conflict with Arianism resulted in his writing much, the most notable being on the Trinity. He also wrote commentaries on St Matthew's Gospel and the Psalms. Hilary died in 367 at Poitiers.

One of Hilary's main values in life was the victory of true Catholic doctrine over Arianism. This aim led him into much writing, and dealings with theologians and councils.

To preserve the faith

Keep us, O Lord,
from useless fighting with words
and grant that we always speak the truth.

Preserve us in the faith, true and undefiled,
so that we may always hold on to
what we professed when we were baptised in the
name of the Father, Son and Holy Spirit.
Grant that we may have you for our Father
and that we live in your Son
and in the fellowship of the Holy Spirit
through the same Jesus Christ our Lord.

Ignatius Loyola

Ignatius was born in Loyola, Spain in 1491. As a young man he was proud to excess, jealous of his personal dignity, fastidious in his dress, a dandy ready to draw his sword if jostled on the sidewalk. He was wounded in battle at Pamplona in northern Spain. During his convalescence, because there was not much of a library at Loyola castle, he began to read the Lives of Christ and the saints. Moved by this, he started to reflect on his life to see what spirits were moving him and to where. He became dissatisfied with his past life and resolved to give himself wholly to God. He spent a year in reflection and solitary prayer. This began to give direction to his life. This time was one of great revelations about God, Jesus Christ and the meaning of life. It was also a period of great temptations to suicide, and despair brought on by scruples. But God guided him, and his experiences were to be invaluable when he came to write his *Spiritual Exercises* and to direct others in the ways of God. He thought first of working in Jerusalem but finally went to Paris where he graduated as Master of Arts, as he felt this would be a better way of serving God.

In Paris, seven students joined themselves to Ignatius. In 1534 they decided to be missionaries to the Muslims in Palestine. When this did not work out, they offered their services to Pope Paul III. They were ordained priests and in 1540 became a new religious order – the Society of Jesus (Jesuits). During the remaining fifteen years of his life, Ignatius directed his order from Rome, enlarged its constitutions and saw its numbers grow to 1,000, spread throughout Europe and to the distant lands of Japan, South America and North Africa. Ignatius died quietly in 1556 still administering his order.

The most important value in Ignatius' life was to discern through prayer any irregularities in one's life, find the will of God and do that which was most for his greater glory. He composed a book of spiritual exercises which were designed to help a person to do this. The giving of spiritual retreats to help people regulate their lives was of great importance to him. He was a man with a great gift for friendship and conversation. His main writings are the *Spiritual Exercises, Constitutions* and many letters to the men and women of his time.

For generosity

Teach us, good Lord,
to serve you as you deserve,
to give and not to count the cost,
to fight and not to heed the wounds,
to toil and not to seek for rest,
to labour and to look for no reward

save that of knowing
that we do your will
through Jesus Christ our Lord.

Self offering

Take and receive, O Lord,
all my liberty,
my memory,
my understanding
and my will,
all that I have and own.
You gave them to me.
They are all yours.
Do with them what you will.
Give me your love and your grace;
these are enough for me.
Then I am rich enough,
I do not ask for more.

Generous response

Lord, you, my creator,
became man out of love for me.
You came from eternal life
to death on a cross
so that by your obedience of love
given to the Father
you might die for my sins.
Teach me, Lord,
what I ought to do for you.

Jerome

Jerome, born about 342, was reared as a Christian and studied at Rome. About 374 he spent some years among the hermits of Syria and was ordained priest at Antioch. From 382 to 385 he worked in Rome as secretary to Pope Damascus, who ordered him to revise the Latin version of the New Testament. He became the leader of a group of women who wished to lead holy and studious lives. He was unpopular with many people because of his hot temper and even his fellow monks at times found him somewhat hard to take. When the Pope died, Jerome settled in Jerusalem with some of his disciples. A hostel was opened and Jerome taught Greek and Latin to the local children. He was engaged in much controversy but finished his work on the Bible in 404. He died in Bethlehem sixteen years later.

Jerome valued the truth, which was his guiding light in all his controversies, although his expression of it was often very strong and his contempt for his opponents was expressed even more strongly. Yet, through his warm humanity, he held the affection of his friends and was very considerate to the weak and the lowly.

Repentance

I am the lost sheep
wandering in the desert.
Search for me, Good Shepherd,
and bring me home again
to your fold.
Do with me what you want

so that I may live with you
all the days of my life
and praise you for all eternity
with those who are with you
in heaven.

John Chrysostom

John Chrysostom was born at Antioch about 347, reared as a Christian and baptised only when he was an adult. His aim in life was to become a lawyer. He lived for some years among the holy men in the mountains until 381 when he joined the clergy of Antioch. In 398 he was elected Archbishop of Constantinople. His courageous and sometimes rash attacks against the misuse of wealth and other evils led to his banishment to Armenia. For greater security he was to be transferred to Spain, but he died on the way there in 407.

John Chrysostom is best remembered for the value he placed on preaching that applied the Scriptures to the ordinary lives of his hearers. He wrote much to explain the books of the Old and New Testaments, especially the letters of St Paul.

Before communion

Grant, O Lord that I may receive
your precious Body and Blood
to make me holy,
to enlighten and strengthen me,
to ease the burden of my many sins,

to protect me from the traps of the devil,
to overcome my sinful and evil habits,
to subdue my wayward urges,
to help me to live your commandments,
to increase in me your divine life,
to bring me into your kingdom.

John Fisher

John Fisher was born in Yorkshire, England in 1469, the son of a cloth dealer. He was educated at Cambridge University from the age of fourteen and became a distinguished scholar. He was ordained a priest in 1491 and became vice-chancellor of the university in 1501. He did much to improve the university in many ways and in 1504 became its chancellor and the Bishop of Rochester. He defended strongly the traditional doctrine of the Real Presence and the Eucharistic Sacrifice against Protestant opponents in other English universities. He also defended the validity of the marriage of Henry VIII to Catherine of Aragon and later the supremacy of the Church and of the Pope. He protested against the King's title of 'Head of the Church in England'. From this on he began to fall out of favour. He refused to take the oath that the King was supreme head of the Church. He was imprisoned in the Tower of London and executed in 1535.

John Fisher valued integrity and the welfare of his diocese.

Repentance

Good Lord, we are the sinners
you came to call to yourself.

We are burdened with the number of our sins.
We are tired because of our wickedness.
Say to us, therefore, Lord: 'Come to me'
and immediately we come.
We humble ourselves and bow down
before the throne of your mercy.
Our only hope is in you.
Remember, Lord, the promise you made
to every sorrowful sinner coming to you
that you would not turn them away
but would refresh them.
We come, therefore, to you, good Lord;
do not turn us away but refresh us
with your grace and your mercy.

Repentance

O Lord my God, look on your creature
whom you have made like yourself
and whom you have also redeemed
with the blood of your Son.
Recognise this likeness.
Help me to put away
all that is not of you.
I ask you to deal justly with me
as you have with many others.
help me as I am about to rise from sin
and come to you,
not because I am your son
but because I am your servant.

John Vianney (Curé of Ars)

John Vianney, born near Lyons in France in 1786, was the son of a farmer. His studies for the priesthood lasted from 1806 until 1815, a long time, for his progress was very slow and there were doubts as to whether he was sufficiently gifted to be able to complete the course for his ordination. He was finally ordained, more for his devotion and good will than for his intellectual gifts. In 1818 he was sent to the lonely village of Ars as parish priest and there he remained until his death forty years later. He was very devoted to his parishioners and their needs. He soon earned a name as a preacher and confessor with great gifts. People flocked from all over France and beyond to visit him. Over the years he was in the habit of spending up to eighteen hours hearing the confessions of those who visited him. He was gifted with great insight into people's problems and was very straightforward in the advice he gave them. The long hours in the confessional, the austerity of his personal life and his constant availability to crowds of people slowly wore him out. He died in his parish of Ars in 1859. He is today the patron of parish clergy.

The prime value in the life of John Vianney was bringing God's graces and light to people in the sacrament of confession, the administration of which took most of his life.

To Our Lady for a happy death

O most holy Virgin Mary, who stands forever
before the most holy Trinity;
and to whom it is granted at all times

to pray for us to your Son;
pray for me in all my needs;
help me; beg and obtain
for me the pardon of all my sins.
Help me especially at my last hour;
and when I can no longer give any sign
of the use of reason, then encourage me;
make the sign of the cross for me
and fight for me against the enemy.
Make in my name an act of faith;
favour me with a sign of my salvation
and never let me despair of the mercy of God.
Help me to defeat the wicked enemy.
When I can no longer say:
'Jesus, Mary and Joseph, I place my soul in
your hands', let you say it for me.
When I can no longer hear human words of
consolation and comfort, let you comfort me.
Do not leave me before I have been judged
and if I have to free my soul from sin in
purgatory, pray for me immediately without
ceasing and inspire my friends to pray for me
so that I may soon enjoy the sight of God.
Lighten my sufferings; deliver me quickly
and lead my soul into heaven with you,
so that united with you and all the saints
I may bless and praise my God for all eternity.

Patrick

Patrick, the apostle of Ireland, was born either in France or England about 385. He was the son of an imperial Roman official. At the age of sixteen, he was taken by pirates to pagan Ireland and sold as a slave to be used for herding sheep. During his lonely herding on the mountains of Ireland, he developed a deep prayer life. Escaping to Europe about 408, he became a monk and was ordained priest. About 432 he returned to Ireland as a missionary bishop. There were already some Christians in Ireland but very little headway had been made. Patrick's widespread preaching helped greatly to organise the Church in Ireland. He died about 461.

Patrick, during his six years of slavery and solitude, began to see the value of religion and became a man of intense prayer and awareness of God's presence, as seen from the *Breastplate of St Patrick* which he is supposed to have written. He also wrote his *Confessions* in which he reviewed his life and work. What stands out in the *Confessions* as a most important value for Patrick is the sense of being called by God to the work of bringing the gospel to many people, 'I owe it to God's grace that so many people should through me be born again'.

God's protection

I rise today through
God's strength to pilot me,
God's eye to look before me,
God's ear to hear me,
God's word to speak for me,
God's hand to guard me,
God's way to lie before me,
God's shield to protect me,
God's hosts to save me

from the snares of the devil,
from everyone who desires me ill
from afar or near,
alone or in a crowd.

Christ's presence

Christ with me,
Christ before me,
Christ behind me,
Christ in me,
Christ beneath me,
Christ above me,
Christ on my right,
Christ on my left,
Christ when I lie down,
Christ when I sit down,
Christ when I arise,
Christ in the heart of everyone
who thinks of me,
Christ in the eye that sees me,
Christ in the ear that hears me.

Peter Canisius

Peter Canisius was born in Holland in 1521. He went to the university of Cologne in Germany to study law, but changed to theology. He became friendly with the Jesuit Peter Favre and, influenced by him, entered the Society of Jesus in 1543. From 1546 to 1562 he preached, attended the Council of Trent, spent six months with St Ignatius Loyola in Rome, taught in the

Jesuit school at Messina and reformed the university at Ingoldstadt in Bavaria. He did similar work in Vienna. He did much writing to strengthen the faith of Catholics against Protestantism and founded many schools, colleges and seminaries before he died at Fribourg in Switzerland in 1597.

Peter Canisius valued most highly the Catholic faith and much of his time and energy were devoted to writing in order to defend it and keep the peoples of South Germany loyal to it. His best known writings are his three *Catechisms of Christian Doctrine* for pupils of different ages. He also gave much of his time to encouraging printers and publishers. Peter Canisius was moderate and understanding, though this, as seen from his prayers, did not come easily to him.

For others

Almighty, everlasting God,
awaken in us that courage
which the first Christians showed
in witnessing their faith;
fervour in prayer,
in reception of the sacraments,
in love of God and other people.
May our work and rest,
our actions and conduct,
our life and death
be entrusted to you, O God.
Grant us your grace here on earth
and let us, in the company of the saved
in heaven, praise, honour and glorify you
in everlasting happiness.

For others

Almighty God, ruler of living and dead,
whose hand holds everything in being,
look graciously on all whom we commend
to your mercy;
those who have authority over us,
our family, relatives, helpers
and all who have claims on us
by reason of relationship or friendship.
Bless our family, our home town, our country,
that men and women there in every walk of life
may live in peace, and freed from sin,
always sincerely seeking by their way of life
to please you.

For the youth

Almighty, everlasting God,
bless our youth
who are exposed to many dangers
to faith and morals.
Grant to young men and women
that in the precious years of their youth
they may not forget
their Creator and Saviour
nor lose their purity of heart.
Receive under your special protection
the children whom you welcomed
when on earth with such tender love
and whom you called blessed.

Polycarp

Polycarp was one of a group known as 'the Apostolic Fathers' who received instruction directly from the apostles. Apart from this, very little is known about Polycarp. He was bishop of Smyrna where he was martyred about 155, having been betrayed by a servant.

For perfection

God and Father,
Jesus, Eternal High Priest,
build us up in faith,
truth and love
and give us our place
among the saints
with all those who believe in you.
We pray for all saints,
for kings and rulers,
for the enemies of Christ's cross
and for ourselves
that our fruit may abound
and we may be made perfect
through you.

Richard

Richard was born at Droitwich in England in 1197. He studied at Paris and Bologna, becoming chancellor of his university in 1235 and shortly afterwards became chancellor of St Edmund's at Canterbury. He was exiled with Edmund and soon after was ordained priest in France. He returned to England and was elected bishop of Chichester in 1244. He spent nine years reforming and running his diocese and died at Dover in England in 1253.

Richard valued integrity in the Church and in his personal life. He spent much of his short life fighting nepotism and simony, the selling of sacred things for money. He was very strict with the priests of his diocese and with himself. He was generous to the poor and was very much at home with the ordinary people of the diocese.

To follow Christ

Thanks to you, my Lord Jesus Christ,
for all the gifts you have won for me,
for all the pains and insults
you have borne for me.
O merciful Redeemer,
friend and brother,
may I know you more clearly,
love you more dearly,
and follow you more nearly,
for ever and ever.

Teresa

Teresa was born in Avila, Spain in 1515. A talented and lively girl from a respected family, she entered the Carmelite convent in her home town when she was about twenty. She found it very hard to leave her family and at first suffered very bad health. The convent in which she found herself was a large and easy-going community which had free contacts with the outside world. Teresa persevered and made great progress in prayer. When she was middle-aged, with the encouragement of St Peter of Alcantara, she decided to found a convent under the original strict form of the Carmelite rule. After many set-backs, the convent was opened at Avila in 1562. For the next twenty years Teresa, as she herself wrote, 'traipsed' up and down Spain founding seventeen convents under conditions of great hardship. Broken in health, she died in 1582.

The prime value in Teresa's life was the combination of deep prayer, intense activity and a joyful, common-sense efficiency in the practical affairs of daily living. Her common sense is humorously illustrated by the story of how one day a visitor found her sitting eating a partridge which she had been given. The visitor was shocked and asked what would people think of a holy woman enjoying her food. Teresa replied that she did not care what people thought, since there was a time for partridge and a time for penance. Her friendly attitude to God in prayer may be gathered from her saying: 'Lord, it is no wonder you have so few friends when you treat the ones you have so badly'. The most important of her many writings are her *Life* (up to 1562), *The Way of Perfection* (instructions for her sisters), *The Book of the Foundations* (a lively account of the establishment of her convents) and *The Interior Castle* (an account of her inner life). For her writings on the spiritual life she was made a Doctor of the Church.

To choose God's will

Rule all by your wisdom, Lord,
so that I may always serve you
according to your will
and not as I may choose.
Do not punish me, I ask you,
by granting that which I wish or ask
if it offends your love.
Because I want your love
to live always in my soul.
Let me deny myself
so that I may serve you
who in yourself are the true life.

To the Lord as a friend

How true it is, Lord,
that you bear with those
who cannot bear you to be with them!
How good a friend you are, my Lord.
You comfort us and suffer and wait
until we become more like you
bearing with us meanwhile as we are.
You remember the times when we love you
and the times when we repent,
you forget the times
when we have offended you.

Grace for the present and future

You know well, my God,
that in all my miseries

I have never failed to recognise
your great power and mercy.
May it help me
that I have not offended in this.
Give me back the time I have lost
by granting me your grace
both in the present
and in the future.

For God's help

Lord, how can someone ask for your help
who has served you so badly
and hardly been able to keep
what you have already given?
How can you have any confidence
in one who has so often betrayed you?
What can I do?
Comfort of the comfortless,
Help of all who look for help from you
tell us to pray to you
and say that you will not fail to give.

To love God above all

O my God, you are charity and love itself
make charity and love grow perfect in me
so that your love may burn up all my self-love.
My only treasure, all my glory,
make me love you more than any created thing
so that I may love myself in you
and love my neighbour

and help him in his difficulties.
Apart from you, let me never love anything else
and may I use all things to go to you
and for nothing else,
I am glad and will be glad
because of the love you have for yourself
in that endless love
that the angels and saints have for you in heaven.
I am glad because your holy servants on earth
who know you by the light of faith
know that you alone are their highest good
and the centre of their love,
I wish that all sinners in this world
should love you in this way
and with your grace I will help them to do so.

Thomas Aquinas

Thomas Aquinas was born near Aquina in Italy about 1225. He was educated by the Benedictines at Monte Cassino and in the university of Naples. In 1244 he joined the Dominican Order, but his rich relatives, angered by his choice of life, kidnapped him and locked him up for a year. But Thomas did not change his mind and, on his release, went to study under St Albert the Great in Paris and in Cologne in Germany. In 1256 he took the degree of Master of Theology. He spent the rest of his life teaching, preaching and, most of all, writing. He died on his way to the General Council of Lyons in 1274.

Thomas Aquinas valued most highly contemplation

of the truth about God, his creation and our behaviour as creatures of God. He is best known for his handing on of the truths of his reflections in clear systematic writings that fill many volumes. His best known theological works are on God and his creation *(Summa contra Gentiles)* and a systematic summary of theology which combined secular philosophy and theology *(Summa Theologica)*. St Thomas' influence on theology has been enormous, even outside the Church.

For a steady heart

Give us, Lord, a steady heart
which no unworthy liking may drag down.
Give us an unconquered heart
which no trouble can wear out.
Give us an upright heart
which no unworthy purpose may turn aside.

For virtues

Make me, Lord,
obedient without complaint,
poor without regret,
patient without murmur,
humble without pretence,
joyful without foolishness,
truthful without disguise.

To seek and do God's will

God of all goodness, grant us
to desire ardently,

to seek wisely,
to know surely,
to accomplish perfectly,
your holy will
for the glory of your name.

God alone

O merciful God,
grant that I may always do your will
perfectly in all things.
May it be my wish to work
only for your honour and glory.
May I rejoice in nothing
except what leads to you.
May I wish nothing
that leads away from you.
May all passing things
be as nothing in my eyes.
May all that is yours be dear to me
and may you, my God, be dear to me
above all things.
May I wish for nothing apart from you.
May all joys have no importance for me
apart from you.
May all effort and work delight me
when it is for you.

Thomas More

Thomas More was born in London in 1478. He became a lawyer in 1501 and entered Parliament in 1504. He married and had three daughters and a son. He was a true humanist, a man of deep learning and human culture. Under King Henry VIII he held many high positions and negotiated many delicate government missions. In 1529 he became Lord Chancellor and as a judge was known for his fairness and incorruptibility. He took a small part defending Catholicism against the new doctrines of Martin Luther. King Henry tried to involve Thomas in procuring a declaration of nullity for his valid marriage to Catherine of Aragon. Thomas refused to take an oath which obliged people to swear that the King rather than the Pope was the head of the Church in England. He retired from the Chancellorship and from public life and was imprisoned in the Tower of London. He was executed in 1535 on a false charge of treason based on his refusal to acknowledge the King as supreme head on earth of the Church in England.

Thomas More is best remembered for his supreme value of following his conscience in complicated circumstances and being prepared to sacrifice all rather than desert God. His statement to the crowd from the gallows best sums up his life when he said that he was 'the king's good servant, but God's first'.

His best known writings are *Utopia* and *A Dialogue of Comfort against Tribulation,* both written during his imprisonment in the Tower of London.

For a good life

Give us, Lord,
a humble, quiet, peaceable,
patient, tender, charitable mind
and in all our thoughts, words and deeds
a taste of your Holy Spirit.

Give us, Lord,
a lively faith,
a firm hope,
a warm charity,
a love of you.
Take from us all lukewarmness in prayer.
Give us warmth and delight
in thinking of you
and your grace and tender compassion to us.
The things that we pray for, Lord,
give us grace to work for,
through Jesus Christ our Lord.

To think of one's last end
Give me grace to amend my life
and to keep my eyes on my last end
without fear of death
which to those who die in you, good Lord,
is the gateway of a wealthy life.